HOMEMADE CANDIES

FUN AND EASY

The Enthusiast publishes books and paper goods. Subjects include, vintage how-to, retro-cooking and home economics, holidays and celebrations, games and puzzles, graphic design, classic children's literature, illustrated literature and poetry, humour.

What's Your Passion?

 Enthusiast.cc

TheEnthusiast@Enthusiast.cc

ISBN / EAN
Standard Edition 1595837507 / 9781595837509

CONTENTS

HINTS ON CANDY MAKING pages 4-5

FUDGE & PENUCHE pages 6-17

FONDANTS & CREAMS pages 18-33

CARAMELS pages 34-39

TOFFEE & BRITTLE pages 40-47

HARD CANDIES pages 48-51

TAFFY pages 52-53

NOUGAT & DIVINITY pages 54-57

GEL CANDIES pages 58-59

PRALINES & MOLASSES pages 60-61

CHIPS & POPCORN pages 62-63

Equipment

1. Cook candy in a smooth saucepan large enough to allow it to boil, holding about 2 to 3 quarts.

2. Any kind of pan can be used, but the candy will not stick as readily in a heavy metal pan as in a thin one and copper pans are ideal.

3. A wooden spoon is best for candy making.

4. A candy thermometer is essential. For best results, follow the temperatures suggested in each candy recipe in this book.

Cooking

1. Cook candies rapidly and stir frequently until sugar dissolves, then lower the heat and cook slowly, stirring occasionally.

2. Granulated sugar should be fine grained and free from specks. If not, crush it with a rolling pin or sift it through a fine sieve before using.

3. Remove the pan from heat when making the "cold water" test. Let candy fall into bowl of cold water in small drops rather than in large ones. When the drops form a:

Soft ball - the hot syrup will stay together in one mass and can be lifted out of the water, but flattens when laid upon the fingers.

Firm ball - the hot syrup will hold its shape when lifted out of the water, yet feels plastic.

Hard ball - the hot syrup separates into threads when it strikes the water, but can be shaped into a ball.

CANDIES

Smith College Fudge

¼ cup butter
1 cup white sugar
1 cup brown sugar
¼ cup molasses
½ cup cream
2 ounces unsweetened chocolate, grated
1 ½ teaspoons vanilla extract

Melt the butter. Mix together in a separate bowl the white sugar, brown sugar, molasses and cream. Add this mixture to the butter. After it has been brought to a boil, continue boiling for two and a half minutes, stirring rapidly. Add the grated chocolate. Boil this five minutes, stirring it first rapidly, and then more slowly towards the end. After it has been removed from heat. Add vanilla. Then stir constantly until the mass thickens. Pour into buttered pan and set in a cool place.

Double Fudge

2 cups of granulated sugar
2 ounces unsweetened chocolate
½ cup of cream
1 tablespoonful of butter.

Mix ingredients together in a bowl. After it has been brought to a boil, continue boiling for seven minutes; then beat and spread in buttered tin to cool.

2 cups of brown sugar
1 teaspoonful of vanilla extract.
½ cup of cream
1 cup of walnut meats chopped fine,
1 tablespoonful of butter.

Mix ingredients together in a bowl. After it has been brought to a boil, continue boiling for ten minutes; then beat and pour on top of fudge already in pan. When cool, cut in squares.

Marbled Fudge

2 cups of granulated sugar
2 ounces unsweetened chocolate, grated
¼ cup of light corn syrup
1 ½ cups of cream
1 tablespoonful of butter for greasing pans, or spray
2 teaspoonfuls of vanilla.

Stir the sugar, pure corn syrup and cream in a saucepan over low heat until the sugar is melted; increase heat and continue stirring until the mixture boils, then let boil, stirring gently every three or four minutes, until the thermometer registers 236° F., or till a soft ball can be formed in cold water. Remove from the heat and pour one-half of the mixture over the chocolate in separate pan or bowl. Set both portions on a cake rack, or on something that will allow the air to circulate. When the mixture cools a little; add a teaspoonful of vanilla to each dish, and beat until thick and slightly grainy, then put the mixture into a greased pan, lined with waxed paper, first a little of one and then of the other, to give a marbled effect. When nearly cold turn from the pan, peel off the paper and cut into cubes.

Fudge Hearts

2 cups of granulated sugar
¼ cup of butter
¼ cup of condensed milk
1 ½ ounces unsweetened chocolate
⅓ a cup of water
1 teaspoonful of vanilla extract

Boil the sugar, milk and water to 236° F., or to the soft-ball degree; stir gently every few minutes; add the butter and let boil up vigorously, then remove from the heat and add the chocolate; let stand undisturbed until cool, then add the vanilla and beat the candy until it thickens and begins to sugar. Pour into a greased pan lined with paper to stand until cooled; turn from the mould and with a heart shaped cookie cutter cut into shapes.

Marshmallow Fudge

1st batch & 2nd batch
2 cups of granulated sugar
1 cup of cream
¼ teaspoonful of salt
1 tablespoonful of butter
2 ounces unsweetened chocolate
1 teaspoonful of vanilla.

1st batch ONLY - half a pound of marshmallows, split in halves.

Start with the first batch and when this is nearly boiled enough, set the second batch to cook, preparing it in the same manner as the first

Stir the sugar and cream, in a saucepan over low heat until the sugar is melted, when the sugar boils wash down the sides of the pan as in making fondant, set in the *marshmallow fudge cont...*

thermometer and cook over high heat, without stirring, to the soft ball degree, 236° F.; add the butter, salt and chocolate, melted or shaved fine, and let boil up vigorously, then remove to a cake cooler (or two spoon handles to allow a circulation of air below the pan).

In the meantime the second batch should be cooking and the marshmallows be gotten ready.

When the first batch is about cold add the vanilla and beat the candy vigorously until it begins to thicken, then turn it into a greased pan lined with waxed paper. Immediately place the halves of marshmallows close together on the top of the fudge.

When the other dish of fudge is ready (as above;) set it into cold water and when nearly cold, add the vanilla and beat as in the first batch, then pour it over the marshmallows. When the whole is about cold turn it onto a marble, or cutting board, pull off the paper and cut into cubes.

NOTE: If one is able to work very quickly, only one batch need be prepared, half of it being spread over the marshmallows.

CANDIES

Chocolate Fudge

2 ounces unsweetened chocolate, cut in pieces
2 cups sugar
Dash of salt
⅔ cup cold milk
2 tablespoons butter
1 teaspoon vanilla

Add chocolate to milk in saucepan and place over low heat. Cook until mixture is smooth and blended, stirring constantly. Add sugar and salt, and stir until sugar is dissolved and mixture boils. Continue cooking, without stirring , until a small amount of mixture forms a very soft ball in cold water (232° F.) Remove from heat. Add butter and vanilla. Cool to lukewarm (110° F.), then beat until mixture begins to thicken and loses its gloss. Pour at once into greased pan, 8 x 4 inches. When cold, cut in squares.

Tutti Frutti Fudge

To make Tutti-frutti Fudge, add 4 tablespoons each candied cherries, candied pineapple, figs, and raisins, finely cut, and 4 tablespoons Pistachio meats, blanched, to Chocolate Fudge, just before pouring it into pan.

Nut Fudge

To make Nut Fudge, add 1 cup broken nut meats to Chocolate Fudge just before pouring it into pan. Halves of walnuts or pecans may be pressed into fudge while still soft in regular arrangement, so that when fudge is cut each piece contains a nut in center of top.

Coconut Fudge

To make Coconut Fudge, cook Chocolate Fudge to 230° F. instead of to 232° F. Add 1 cup grated coconut, just before pouring it into pan. In cutting coconut fudge, use very sharp knife.

Cocoa Fudge

½ a cup of milk
6 tablespoonfuls of unsweetened cocoa
3 tablespoonfuls of butter
Pinch of salt
2 ½ cups of powdered sugar
1 teaspoonful of vanilla

Mix all ingredients together in a saucepan, but vanilla; cook, stirring constantly, until it begins to boil, then cook slowly, stirring occasionally, eight or ten minutes, until the thermometer registers 236° F or until it makes a firm ball when dropped in cold water. When cooked enough, add the vanilla and beat until it seems like very cold molasses in winter. Pour into a buttered pan; when firm, cut in squares. Great care must be taken not to beat too much, because it cannot be poured into the pan, and will not have a gloss on top.

Chocolate Dipped Fruit Fudge

1 ½ cups of granulated sugar
1 cup of maple syrup
1 ½ cups of light corn syrup
½ cup of heavy cream
⅓ cup of milk
¼ cup butter
¾ cup of fruit, figs, candied cherries and apricots, cut in small pieces
1 cup melted dipping chocolate

Stir together the sugar, maple syrup, corn syrup, milk, butter and cream until the sugar is melted, cover and let boil three or four minutes, then uncover and let boil, stirring gently until a soft ball may be formed in cold water, or until the thermometer registers 236° F. Set the saucepan on a cake cooler and when the mixture becomes cool, add the fruit and beat until it becomes thick, then turn into pans lined with waxed paper. In about fifteen minutes cut into squares. Coat these with the dipping chocolate, adding more as desired.

Peanut Butter Fudge

2 cups sugar
⅔ cup milk
4 tablespoons peanut butter
1 teaspoon vanilla
Few grains salt

Put sugar and milk in saucepan, bring to the boiling point and let boil, stirring gently until a soft ball may be formed in cold water, or until the thermometer registers 236° F. Remove from range, add remaining ingredients and beat until creamy. Turn into a buttered pan to three-fourths inch in depth, cool slightly and cut in squares.

Penuche

2 cups light brown sugar
⅔ cup milk
1 tablespoon butter
1 teaspoon vanilla
1 cup chopped nuts

penuche cont...

In a sauce pan, add sugar and milk. Bring to a boil and stirring constantly bring temperature to a soft-ball stage, 236°F. Remove from heat, add butter but do not stir. Set aside to cool to lukewarm, 110°F. Add in vanilla and beat until the mixture is smooth, thick and creamy. Add in the nuts. Pour into greased pan and cut into squares when cold.

Coffee Penuche

2 cups light brown sugar
⅔ cup coffee
1 tablespoon butter
1 teaspoon vanilla
1 cup chopped nuts

In a sauce pan, add sugar and milk. Bring to a boil and stirring constantly bring temperature to a soft-ball stage, 236°F. Remove from heat, add butter but do not stir. Set aside to cool to lukewarm, 110°F. Add in vanilla and beat until the mixture is smooth, thick and creamy. Add in the nuts. Pour into greased pan and cut into squares when cold.

How to Make Fondant

Fondant is the perfect base for real chocolate creams. Good fondant is creamy and smooth because it contains innumerable tiny sugar crystals, so small that they cannot be felt on the tongue. It should be made at least 24 hours before using for, on standing, it becomes smoother in texture and can be more easily kneaded. This process is known as "ripening." There are three main types of fondant. Plain water fondant, white and creamy, is a simple starting point for many delightful centers. Cream fondant, rich and smooth textured, is excellent with fruits and nuts. And in chocolate fondant, the full and mellow flavor of chocolate is blended into a luscious base for plain chocolate creams or delectable French creams.

Water Fondant

2 cups sugar
Dash of salt
2 tablespoons light corn syrup
¾ cup boiling water
½ teaspoon vanilla

water fondant cont...

Combine ingredients (except vanilla) in deep 2 quart saucepan. Place over low flame and stir constantly until sugar is dissolved and mixture boils. Cover and cook 3 minutes; then remove cover and continue cooking, without stirring, until a small amount of syrup forms a soft ball in cold water (240° F.). During cooking, wash down sides of pan occasionally with damp cloth. Pour fondant at once on cold, wet baking sheet or marble slab. Cool to lukewarm (110° F.) and work with broad spatula or wooden paddle until white and creamy. Then knead in the hands until smooth; add vanilla and knead until vanilla is blended. Let stand, uncovered, until cold; then wrap in waxed paper and store in tightly covered jar in refrigerator or other cool place to ripen for at least 24 hours before using. Fondant may be kept for several weeks. If during storage period it becomes too dry to use, cover it with a damp cloth. Makes about one pound fondant.

❀

Cream Fondant

Prepare as for Water Fondant above, substituting heavy cream in the place of the boiling water.

Chocolate Fondant

3 ounces unsweetened chocolate
¾ cup water
2 cups sugar
Dash of salt
2 tablespoons light corn syrup
½ teaspoon vanilla

Add chocolate to water in deep 2 quart saucepan and place over low flame. Cook until mixture is smooth and blended, stirring constantly. Add sugar, salt, and corn syrup, and stir until sugar is dissolved and mixture boils. Cover and cook 3 minutes; then remove cover and continue cooking, without stirring, until a small amount of syrup forms a soft ball in cold water (236° F.). During cooking, wash down sides of pan occasionally with damp cloth. Pour fondant at once on cold, wet baking sheet or marble slab. Cool to lukewarm (110° F.) and work with broad spatula or wooden paddle until creamy. Then knead in the hands until smooth; add vanilla and knead until vanilla is blended. Let stand, uncovered, until cold; then wrap in waxed paper and store as for Water Fondant (above). Makes about 1 pound.

To Mould Candy in Starch Impressions

Many candies, especially those that are of some variety of fondant, are thin when warm and solidify on the outside when cold, so that they may be "dipped" or coated with chocolate.

To shape candy of this sort, fill a low pan with cornstarch, making it smooth upon the top. Press a thimble, round piece of wood, or the stopper of an oil or vinegar cruet into the cornstarch; lift from the starch and repeat the impressions as many times as the space allows.

Pour candy into the impressions, and when firm, lift out and simply dust off the corn starch with a brush.

Chocolate Butter Creams

2 ½ cups of sugar
2 ½ ounces of unsweetened chocolate
½ cup water
½ cup light corn syrup
2 teaspoonfuls of vanilla
¼ a cup of butter
½ pound of dipping chocolate

Heat the sugar, water, corn syrup and butter; stir until the sugar is melted, then cook to the soft ball degree, or 236° F.; pour on a damp marble or baking sheet, leave until cold; then pour on the chocolate, melted over hot water, and with a spatula turn to a cream. Cover the chocolate fondant with a bowl and let stand for thirty minutes; knead well and set over a double boiler; add the vanilla and stir until melted. The mixture is now ready to be dropped into small impressions in cornstarch; when cold brush off cornstarch, dip in dipping chocolate. When dropping the mixture into the starch it should be soft enough to run level on the top. If too soft it will not hold its shape in coating.

Surprise Chocolate Creams

Use Water Fondant recipe from page 18
Chopped peanuts,
Candied or maraschino cherries
½ a pound of dipping chocolate
Flavoring of almond or vanilla

Melt the fondant over hot water and add the flavoring. Put a bit of cherry in the bottom of each starch impression, then turn in the melted fondant, to fill the impressions and have them level on the top. Let the chocolate, broken in bits, be melted over warm water, then add as many chopped peanuts as can be well stirred into it; let cool to about 80° F. and in it drop the creams, one at a time; as coated place them on waxed paper.

Walnut Cream Chocolates

2 ½ cups of granulated sugar
½ a cup of condensed milk
1 teaspoonful of vanilla,
½ a cup of water
3 or 4 tablespoonfuls of caramel syrup
A little water
½ a pound of dipping chocolate
30-40 walnut pieces

Cook the sugar, condensed milk and water in a saucepan to boil, stir gently but often, and let cook to the soft ball stage, or to 238° F. Pour on a damp marble or baking sheet and let stand undisturbed until cold; turn to a cream, then gather into a compact mass; cover with a bowl and let stand for thirty minutes; then knead the cream; put it into a double boiler; add the caramel syrup and the vanilla; stir constantly while the mixture becomes warm and thin; add

walnut cream chocolates cont...

a tablespoonful or two of water, if necessary, and drop the cream mixture into impressions made in cornstarch. Use two teaspoons to drop the cream. When the candy is cold, pick it from the starch. With a small brush remove the starch that sticks to the candy shapes. Coat each piece with dipping chocolate. As each piece is coated and dropped onto wax paper, set half a walnut meat upon the top

Chocolate Almond Bars

½ cup of sugar
½ cup of blanched almonds, chopped fine
¾ cup of light corn syrup
⅓ recipe for chocolate fondant
¼ cup of water,
3 or 4 ounces of unsweetened chocolate,
1 teaspoonful of vanilla.

Melt the sugar in the water and corn syrup and let boil to about 252° F. , or between a soft and a hard ball. Add the almonds and the vanilla, mix thoroughly and turn onto a marble or baking sheet over which powdered sugar has been sifted. Turn out the candy in such a way that it will take a rectangular shape. When cool enough score it in strips about an inch and a quarter wide, and, as it grows cooler, lift the strips, one by one, to a board and cut them in pieces half or three-quarters of an inch wide. When cold, drop them, sugar side down, in chocolate fondant prepared for "dipping. With the fork push them below the fondant, lift out, drain as much as possible, and set onto wax paper.

Chocolate Peppermint Candy

Use Water Fondant recipe from page 18

Melt a little fondant and flavor it to taste with essence of peppermint; leave the mixture white or tint very delicately with green or pink color-paste. With a teaspoon drop the mixture onto waxed paper to make rounds of the same size—about one inch and a quarter in diameter—let these stand in a cool place about one hour. Put about a cup of fondant in a double boiler, add two ounces of chocolate and a teaspoonful of boiling water, then stir (over hot water) until the fondant and chocolate are melted and evenly mixed together; then drop the peppermints, one by one, into the chocolate mixture, and remove them with the fork to a piece of wax paper; let stand until the chocolate is set, when they are ready to use.

Fondant for Soft Chocolate Creams

2 ½ cups of sugar
1 cup of water
⅓ cup of light corn syrup

Heat the sugar, pure corn syrup and water until boiling, then wash down the sides of the saucepan, cover and finish cooking as in making ordinary fondant. Let cook to 238° F. Turn the syrup onto a damp marble or platter and before it becomes cold turn to a cream with a wooden spatula. When the fondant begins to stiffen, scrape at once into a bowl and cover with a damp cloth, but do not let the cloth touch the fondant. Use in the following recipes.

Rose Chocolate Creams

Fondant for soft chocolate creams above
1 teaspoon of rose extract

rose chocolate creams cont...

Red food color
½ pound of dipping chocolate

Put the fondant into a double boiler over boiling water. Add a little food color to the fondant; add the extract and stir until the mixture is hot, thin and evenly tinted. With two teaspoons drop the mixture into impressions made in starch; it should be hot and thin enough to run level on top. When the shapes are cold, remove from the starch, brush carefully and coat with chocolate.

Pistachio Chocolate Creams

Fondant for soft chocolate creams at left
⅓ a teaspoonful of almond extract
Green food color
Pistachio nuts in slices and halves,
1 teaspoonful of vanilla extract,
½ pound dipping chocolate.

Using green color-paste, vanilla and almond extract, mould the fondant in long shapes. Put a bit of nut in each impression, before filling it with fondant. When firm coat with dipping chocolate and set half a pistachio nut on top.

Almond Fondant Sticks

2 ½ cups granulated sugar
¼ pound unsweetened chocolate
¼ cup of light corn syrup,
1 teaspoon vanilla extract
½ a cup of water
½ pound of dipping chocolate
¼ pound of almond paste

Put the sugar, pure corn syrup and water over the heat. Stir until the sugar is dissolved. Wash down the sides of the kettle as in making fondant. Let boil to the soft ball degree, or to 238° F. Add the almond paste, cut into small, thin pieces, let boil up vigorously, then turn onto a damp marble. When nearly cold turn to a cream with wooden spatula. It will take considerable time to turn this mixture to fondant. Cover and let stand half an hour. Add the

almond fondant sticks cont...

baking chocolate, melted over hot water, and knead it in thoroughly. Add at the same time the vanilla. The chocolate must be added warm. At once cut off a portion of the fondant and knead it into a round ball; then roll it lightly under the fingers into a long strip the shape and size of a lead pencil; form as many of these strips as desired; cut the strips into two-inch lengths and let stand to become firm. Have ready the dipping chocolate melted over hot water and in this coat the prepared sticks, leaving the surface a little rough.

Almond Fondant Balls

Roll part of the almond fondant into small balls. Some of the dipping chocolate will be left after dipping the almond chocolate sticks. Remelt this over hot water, and in it coat the balls lightly. As each ball is coated with the chocolate drop it onto a plate of chopped pistachio nut meats or of shredded cocoanut. With a spoon sprinkle the chopped material over the balls.

Maple Fondant Acorns

2 cups of maple syrup
2 ounces unsweetened chocolate
1¾ cups of granulated sugar
¾ a cup of cold water
1 teaspoonful of vanilla,
Confectioner's sugar
About ¼ a cup of fine-chopped almonds, browned in the oven.

Make fondant of the syrup, granulated sugar and cold water, following the directions given for fondant made of granulated sugar (cream of tartar or other acid is not required in maple fondant.) Work some of the fondant, adding confectioner's sugar as needed, into cone shapes; let these stand an hour or longer to harden upon the outside. Put a little of the fondant in a dish over hot water; add *maple fondant acorns cont...*

chocolate and vanilla as desired and beat till the chocolate is evenly mixed through the fondant, then dip the cones in the chocolate and set them on a piece of waxed paper. When all are dipped, lift the first one dipped from the paper and dip the base again in the chocolate, and then in the chopped-and-browned almonds. Continue till all have been dipped.

WALTER BAKER & CO'S
PREMIUM NO. 1 CHOCOLATE

FAC-SIMILE OF ½ LB. PACKAGE.

CANDIES

Chocolate Caramel Walnuts

White of 1 egg
1 teaspoonful of vanilla extract,
3 tablespoonfuls of maple or caramel syrup
2 ounces of unsweetened chocolate,
1 tablespoonful of water
Walnuts
Sifted confectioner's sugar

Beat the white of egg slightly, add the syrup, water, sugar as needed, the chocolate, melted over hot water, and the vanilla, also more water if necessary. Work with a knife and knead until thoroughly mixed, then break off small pieces of uniform size and roll them into balls, in the hollow of the hand, flatten the balls a little, set the half of a walnut upon each, pressing the nut into the candy and thus flattening it still more.

Chocolate Caramels

2 ½ cups of sugar
2 ½ cups of whole milk
¾ a cup of pure corn syrup
2 ½ ounces unsweetened chocolate
½ a cup of butter
⅛ a teaspoonful of cream of tartar
1 teaspoonful of vanilla extract

Put the sugar, pure corn syrup, butter, cream of tartar and one cup of the milk over the fire, stir constantly, and when the mass has boiled a few moments, gradually stir in the rest of the milk. Do not let the mixture stop boiling while the milk is being added. Stir every few moments and cook to 248° F., or until, when tested in cold water, a hard ball may be formed; add the chocolate and vanilla and beat them thoroughly through the candy, then turn it into two greased pans. When nearly cold cut into squares.

Chocolate Nut Caramels

2 cups of granulated sugar
3 or 4 squares of unsweetened chocolate
1 ½ cups light corn syrup
2 cups of cream
1½ cups of walnut meats.
1 cup of butter
2 teaspoonfuls of vanilla extract.

Cook the sugar, pure corn syrup, one cup of the cream, and the butter, stirring until the mixture boils vigorously, then gradually add the other cup of cream. Do not allow the mixture to stop boiling while the cream is being added. Cook until the thermometer registers 250° F., stirring gently—move the thermometer, to stir beneath it—every four or five minutes. Remove from heat, add the chocolate and nuts and beat until the chocolate is melted; beat in the vanilla and turn into an oiled pan,, to make a sheet three-fourths an inch thick. When nearly cold turn from the pan and cut into cubes

Milk Caramels

2 cups sugar
1 cup light corn syrup
3 cups milk
¼ cup butter
½ teaspoon salt
1 teaspoon vanilla extract

Heat sugar and syrup in one cup of milk, stirring until dissolved. Then cook, stirring frequently, to 246°- 248° F, or to the firm—ball stage. Slowly add the second cup of milk, and repeat the cooking process. Add the final cup of milk, the butter and salt, and cook to 246°-248° F, or until a ball tested in cold water is of the firmness desired in the finished caramel. Remove from heat, add vanilla extract and pour at once into a buttered pan, marking in squares when cool. Add chopped nuts or coconut if desired.

Ribbon Caramels

Chocolate Layer:

1 teaspoonful of vanilla extract.
1 ¼ cups of granulated sugar,
½ a cup of pure corn syrup
¼ a cup of butter
1⁄16 a teaspoonful of cream of tartar
1 ¼ cups of milk
1 ¼ ounces unsweetened chocolate

White Layer:

⅔ a cup of granulated sugar
¼ a cup of water.
1⁄16 a teaspoonful of cream of tartar
1 cup, less one tablespoonful, of corn syrup,
½ a pound of desiccated cocoanut

ribbon caramels cont...

Put the sugar, pure corn syrup, butter, cream of tartar and the fourth a cup of milk over the fire, stir until the mixture boils, then very gradually stir in the rest of the milk. Let cook, stirring occasionally, to 248° F., or until, when tested in water or on a cold marble, a pretty firm ball may be formed. Add the chocolate and vanilla, mix thoroughly, and turn into two well-buttered shallow pans. For the white layer, put the sugar, water and pure corn syrup over the fire, stir until boiling, then add the cocoanut and stir occasionally until a soft ball may be formed when a little of the mixture is dropped upon a cold marble. Put this mixture over the fire, to dissolve the sugar, but do not let it begin to boil until the chocolate layers are turned into the pans. When the white mixture is ready, turn enough of it onto one of the chocolate layers to make a layer about one-third an inch thick. Have the other chocolate layer cooled, by standing in cold water; remove it from the pan and dispose above the cocoanut layer. Let stand until cold and firm, then cut in cubes; wrap each cube in waxed paper.

CANDIES

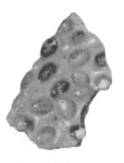

Peanut Brittle

2 tablespoons tasteless vegetable oil, such as safflower oil
2 cups sugar
1 cup water
1 teaspoon cream of tartar
2 cups toasted, salted peanuts

Coat a baking sheet with vegetable oil; set aside. In a heavy-bottomed saucepan over high heat, cook sugar, water and cream of tartar until it is a medium caramel color. Brush down sides of pan with pastry brush dipped in warm water two times to prevent sugar from crystallizing. Add peanuts and stir with wooden spoon to coat them completely with the caramel. Remove the pan from heat, pour the mixture onto the oiled baking sheet and spread it out with wooden spoon. Work very fast, because mixture sets up rapidly. Let the peanut brittle cool completely(about 30 minutes), then break into pieces with your hands.

Any nut may be substituted for the peanuts.

Chocolate Peanut Brittle

1 ½ cups of sugar
1 teaspoonful of vanilla extract,
⅔ a cup of water
1 level teaspoonful of soda,
½ a cup of pure corn syrup
1 tablespoonful of cold water,
2 level tablespoonfuls of butter
½ a pound or more of dipping chocolate
½ a pound of raw shelled peanuts

Cook the sugar, water and pure corn syrup until the sugar is dissolved; wash down the sides of the saucepan with a cloth or the fingers dipped in cold water, cover and let boil three or four minutes, then uncover and let cook to 275° F. (when a little is cooled and chewed it clings but does not stick to the teeth) add the butter and peanuts and stir constantly until the peanuts are nicely browned. Dissolve the soda in the cold water, add the vanilla and the soda and stir vigorously. When the candy is through foaming, turn it onto a warm and well-oiled marble or platter. As soon as it has cooled a little on the edges, take hold of it at the edge and pull out as thin as possible. Loosen it from the receptacle at the center by running a spatula under it, then turn the whole sheet upside down, and again pull as thin as possible. Break into small pieces and when cold coat with melted chocolate.

Almond Toffee

2 cups sugar
3 tablespoons butter
1 ⅓ cups corn syrup
1 teaspoon vanilla
1 ½ cups milk
⅛ teaspoon salt
1 cup blanched almonds

Add sugar, salt, and syrup to milk. Stir until well dissolved. Cook to 270° F., stirring often to prevent scorching. Add butter and cook to 290° F. Remove from stove; add vanilla. Line a well-buttered dish with blanched almonds which should be first browned in an oven. Pour the syrup over this. Mark off in squares while still warm.

When cold, a very thin layer of cocoa butter frosting can be spread over it, and then generously sprinkled over with very finely chopped nuts. Then break apart into pieces with your hands.

American Toffee

2 cups brown sugar
¼ cup butter
½ cup corn syrup
1 cup salted almonds

Heat sugar, butter, and syrup slowly until melted; stir until sugar is dissolved; then boil without stirring to 270° F. Line a well-buttered dish with almonds, removing as much salt as possible. Pour over the hot syrup.
When cold cut in squares. Then break into pieces with your hands.

Storage: In a tightly covered container, the brittle will keep approximately one week at room temperature

CANDIES

Cream Toffee

2 cups brown sugar
1 small can condensed milk
5 tablespoons corn syrup
½ cup butter
1 cup roasted almonds

Cook all ingredients together except almonds, to from 285°
to 295° F. Remove from fire; allow to cool; add almonds;
beat slightly; pour out on buttered plate, and mark off in
squares.

Toffee

1 cup sugar
½ teaspoon ginger
1 cup brown sugar
1 cup water
1½ cup corn syrup
1 teaspoon vanilla
6 tablespoons butter

toffee continued...

1 cup Brazil nuts, filberts, or almonds. Cook all ingredients together, except vanilla and nuts, to 'crack stage', 280° F. Add vanilla and nuts. Pour into a well-buttered pan so that mixture will be about one inch in thickness. Cut in squares and wrap in paper.

❀

Easy Toffee

½ cup butter melted
¾ cup packed brown sugar
½ cup semisweet chocolate pieces
1 cup chopped walnuts

In a 1 ½ quart saucepan combine butter and brown sugar. Cook over medium heat to soft-crack stage or till candy thermometer registers 290°, stirring often. Remove from heat and spread into a buttered 8x8x2-inch baking pan Sprinkle chocolate pieces atop. Let stand 1 to 2 minutes. When chocolate is softened, spread evenly over toffee and sprinkle walnuts atop. Chill thoroughly; break into pieces

Butterscotch Pecan Patties

1 cup sugar
½ cup light brown sugar
⅓ cup light corn syrup
½ cup evaporated milk
⅓ cup butter
¾ pecans pieces
1 teaspoon vanilla

Mix sugars, corn syrup and evaporated milk together in saucepan Cook to boiling point, stirring constantly, Continue cooking, stirring occasionally, to 238° F., or until a few drops form a soft ball when dropped Into cold water, Remove from heat, add butter Cool at room temperature, without stirring, until lukewarm or until the hand can be held comfortably on bottom of pan. Add nuts and vanilla. Beat until candy will hold its shape, Drop from a teaspoon onto waxed paper.

Butterscotch Squares

1 ⅔ cups light brown sugar
⅔ corn syrup
½ cup water
1 ½ tablespoons butter
¼ teaspoon salt
Oil of lemon

Put sugar, corn syrup, and water in a saucepan, stir until is dissolved, bring to boiling point, and boil to 280° F., or until it cracks in cold water. Add butter and salt, and boil to 290° F., or until it reaches the hard crack when tried in cold water. Remove from fire, flavor with oil of lemon, and pour out between bars on slightly moistened slab, mark the squares, and break up when cold.

Lollipops

1 cup sugar
2 to 3 drops wintergreen, peppermint or lemon oil extract
⅔ cup water
⅓ cup light corn syrup
2 to 3 drops food coloring

Put sugar, water and corn syrup in a saucepan. Cook, stirring only until sugar is melted, until temperature reaches 290° F., or until a few drops of the mixture become brittle when dropped into cold water. Remove from heat, add coloring and flavoring. Stir only enough to mix color and extract or candy will sugar. Grease molds or bottom of level pan with mineral oil; it gives hard candy an excellent glaze. Make lollipops quickly by dropping syrup from a spoon into greased molds or flat pan. Press ends of wooden skewers or toothpicks into lollipops immediately after pouring. As soon as they are firm, loosen lollipops from pan or

lollipops cont...

mold. If allowed to remain on pan too long they may crack while being removed. Makes 10 to 12 small lollipops. Note: Decorate with jelly beans, raisins, nuts, candies, or cherries. Have decorations ready when lollipops are poured and press securely before candy hardens. Good flavor and color combinations are:

Oil of clove or cinnamon, red coloring.
Oil of lime or mint, green coloring
Oil of wintergreen, pink coloring
Oil of lemon, yellow coloring
Oil of orange, orange coloring

You can make colored sugar by adding a drop or two of food coloring to ½ cup granulated sugar, blending well with a fork and drying on waxed paper overnight.

Stick-Jaw

3 cups granulated sugar
3 cups brown sugar
6 tablespoons glucose
4 cups water
1 teaspoon almond extract
1 teaspoon vanilla extract
4 cups shredded coconut

Place the sugars, glucose and water in a large saucepan and cook to 312°, or to the hard crack stage. Add the extracts and coconut. Pour into an oiled platter and when cold, cut into squares.

❀

Barley Sugar

3 cups sugar
2 cups water
1 lemon
Pinch cream of tartar

Dissolve the sugar in the water;then add the thin rind of the lemon and the cream of tartar. Cook to 240°, or to the soft-ball stage, then remove the lemon rind. Add the strained juice of the lemon and cook to 310°, or to the hard-crack stage, taking care that the sirup does not burn. Syrup should be a delicate straw color. Pour onto a well-buttered platter or slab and when candy begins to set, cut in strips. When cool enough to handle, twist each strip. Keep in an airtight container.

Atlantic City Taffy

2 cups sugar
1 cup light corn syrup
1 ½ cups water
2 teaspoons glycerin
2 tablespoons butter
2 teaspoons vanilla
1 ½ teaspoons salt

Combine the sugar, syrup, water, salt and glycerin in a 3-quart heavy saucepan. Place over low heat and stir until sugar dissolves, then cook without stirring to 260° F on candy thermometer or to the hard-ball stage. Remove from the heat and add the butter, stirring until butter is melted. Pour into a buttered 13 x 9-inch shallow pan. Cool until easily handled, then gather into a ball and pull until rather firm. Add the vanilla while pulling, then stretch out into a long rope and cut in 1 or 2-inch pieces. Wrap each piece in waxed paper when hard and twist paper at both ends.

Peanut Butter Taffy

¾ cup sugar
1 cup maple syrup
½ cup corn syrup
¼ teaspoon salt
⅓ cup water
2 ounces chocolate, melted
¼ cup peanut butter

Combine the sugar, syrups, salt and water and cook over low heat, stirring constantly until sugar is dissolved. Cook to 238° F degrees on candy thermometer, then add the chocolate. Pour into a greased pan and cool until easily handled. Pull until almost firm, then spread with the peanut butter. Fold over and pull enough to mix peanut butter thoroughly with candy. Cut into parts and wrap each piece in waxed paper.

❁

Divinity

2 cups sugar
½ cup light corn syrup
¼ teaspoon salt
½ cup hot water
2 egg whites
1 teaspoon vanilla extract

Dissolve sugar syrup, and salt in the hot water. Cook without stirring, to 248°, or to the firm ball stage; wash down with a damp cloth any crystals that may form on the sides of the pan during cooking. Remove from heat and pour gradually over the stiffly beaten egg whites, beating Constantly with a wire whisk. Add extract and continue beating until mixture will hold its shape when dropped from a spoon. Drop by teaspoonfuls on waxed paper or spread into a buttered pan and mark in squares.

Note: Should the divinity become too stiff to manipulate, add a few drops of hot water to bring it back to spreading consistency. If for some reason the divinity does not harden, cook it over hot water until mixture will hold its shape. Chopped nuts, shredded coconut, or dried or candied fruits add interest to divinity and should be added during the beating process.

Sea Foam

3 cups light brown sugar
¼ teaspoon salt
¾ cup water
2 egg whites
1 teaspoon vanilla extract

Dissolve the sugar and salt in the water. Cook, without stirring, to 255°, or to the hard-ball stage. Remove from heat and pour gradually over beaten egg whites, beating constantly. Add vanilla extract. Continue beating until candy cools and will hold its shape. Then drop by spoonfuls on waxed paper, or spread into buttered pan and mark in squares.

Nougat

½ cup blanched filberts
½ cup blanched almonds
¼ cup water
2 cups sugar
1 cup light corn syrup
½ cup honey
¼ teaspoon salt
2 egg whites
2 teaspoons vanilla extract
¼ cup soft butter
¼ cup coarsely chopped candied cherries and/or other candied fruit

Preheat oven to 350° F. Spread filberts and almonds on cookie sheet Toast in oven 10 minutes—just until golden. Set aside. In heavy, straight-side, 3-quart saucepan, combine sugar, corn syrup, honey, salt, and water. Stir, over medium heat, until sugar is dissolved. Continue cooking,

nougat cont...

without stirring, to 252° F on candy thermometer, or until a small amount in cold water forms a hard ball. Meanwhile, in large bowl of electric mixer, at high speed, beat egg whites until stiff peaks form when beaters are slowly raised. In a thin stream, pour about one fourth of hot syrup over egg whites, beating constantly, at high speed, until mixture is stiff enough to hold its shape. Continue cooking rest of syrup to 300° F on candy thermometer, or until a small amount in cold water forms threads. In a thin stream, pour hot syrup over meringue, beating constantly, at high speed, until mixture is stiff enough to hold its shape. Add vanilla and butter, beating until thickened again. With wooden spoon, stir in filberts, almonds, and cherries. Turn mixture into a buttered 11 -by-7-by-1 ¼-inch pan; smooth top with a spatula. Let stand, uncovered, in a cool place overnight; or refrigerate until firm. Loosen edge of candy all around; turn out in large block. With sharp knife, cut into 1 inch pieces. Wrap each piece individually in waxed paper; store in the refrigerator.

Makes about 2 pounds

Dainties

1 cup cold water
1 ½ cups boiling water
4 cups sugar
¼ teaspoonful salt
4 envelopes gelatine
Food coloring
½ teaspoonful peppermint extract
1 teaspoonful cinnamon extract

Heat sugar, salt and boiling water to boiling point. Pour cold water in bowl and sprinkle gelatine on top of water. Add to hot syrup and stir until dissolved. Boil slowly for 15 minutes. Remove from fire and divide into two equal parts. Color one part a delicate red and flavor with cinnamon extract; color the other part a delicate green and flavor with peppermint extract. Rinse two pans (size about 8x4 inches) in cold water, and pour in candy mixture to the

depth of about three-fourths inch and put in a cool place (not a refrigerator), allowing candy to thicken for at least twelve hours. With a wet sharp knife loosen around edges of pan, turn out on board lightly covered with powdered sugar. Cut into cubes and roll in powdered or fine granulated sugar.

NOTE: If lemon flavor is desired, add three tablespoonfuls lemon juice and two teaspoonfuls lemon extract to one part of the candy and leave it uncolored. Any preferred flavoring or coloring may be used. This candy may be made by using 10 drops of oil of cinnamon or cloves instead of the extract. This must be stirred into the mixture thoroughly while it is hot. It may also be made by using 1 teaspoonful ground cinnamon or cloves instead of the extract. In this case the ground spice is boiled with the sugar and water. Candies, however, are not as attractive as when made with extracts or oils.

New Orleans Pralines

1 cup brown sugar
½ cup molasses
1 cup cream
2 tablespoons butter
½ teaspoon vanilla
1 pint pecan nut meats

Boil the first four ingredients, stirring constantly, to 238° F. or until when tried in cold water a soft hall is formed. Add vanilla, pour over the nuts and stir until it begins to sugar.

Drop from tip of spoon in small piles on buttered pans.

Old Time Molasses Candy

½ cup dark brown sugar
1 ½ cups molasses
1 tablespoon butter
1 tablespoon vinegar
1 teaspoon baking soda

Boil first four ingredients to 260° F. or until a drop in cold water forms a hard ball. Then add baking soda while stirring rapidly. Turn at once into flat, buttered pan and if desired spread broken peanuts over the top.

Allow to cool. Then break into pieces for serving.

Potato Chip Candy

1 sweet chocolate bar, 8 oz.
1 cup crumbled potato chips
½ cup of your favorite nut meats, chopped

Melt chocolate bar in double boiler, add the potato chips and nut meats. Mix together well and drop a teaspoonful at a time on a tray. Chill in the refrigerator for 30 minutes, and it's ready to eat. This candy will keep well but it must be kept in a cool place.

Chocolate Popcorn Balls

1 ½ cups sugar
⅔ cup water
½ cup light corn syrup
⅓ cup molasses
3 tablespoons butter
3 ounces unsweetened chocolate, melted
1 teaspoon vanilla
4 quarts pop corn, warmed and salted

Combine sugar, water, and corn syrup. Place over low heat, stir constantly until sugar is dissolved and mixture boils, wash down sides of pan occasionally with wet cloth. Cover, boil 3 to 4 minutes. Uncover, and cook without stirring, until a small amount of syrup forms a hard ball in cold water (270° F) Add molasses and butter, continue cooking, stirring constantly, until a small amount of syrup becomes brittle in cold water (290° F.). Remove from heat. When bubbling ceases, add chocolate and vanilla, blend. Pour over popcorn, mix well. Roll lightly with buttered hands into 2-inch balls.

CPSIA information can be obtained at www.ICGtesting.com
Printed in the USA
LVOW01s1538030414

380209LV00006B/44/P